GOD, LISTEN!

"Prayers That God Always Answers"

John Marshall

God, Listen! – Prayers That God Always Answers
By John Marshall

ISBN 0-9740693-4-5

Copyright © 2003 by John Marshall
Printed in the United States of America

This book or parts thereof may not be reproduced in any form, stored in a retrieval system, or transmitted in any form by any means—electronic, mechanical, photocopy, recording, or otherwise—without prior written permission of the publisher, except as provided by United States copyright law.

Unless otherwise noted, all Scripture quotations are from the New American Standard Version of the Bible. Copyright © 1960, 1962, 1963, 1968, 1971, 1972, 1973, 1975, 1977, 1995 by the Lockman Foundation, a Corporation Not for Profit

Text layout and design by Cathleen Kwas, CLicK Services, Lake Mary Florida.

DEDICATION

I dedicate this book to my precious wife, Priscilla Ann Jackson Marshall. Through her, I came face-to-face with the awesomeness, yet simplicity of New Testament, non-denominational Christianity. Therefore, I owe the igniting of my spiritual passion to her.

Priscilla has woven herself into the very spiritual cloth that covers me, just as prayer weaves itself into the very fabric of the Christian lifestyle. For the past twenty-five years, she has traversed the tug-of-war tunnels without hesitation or reservation. The very essence of who she is resonates throughout the crevices of my life.

Priscilla has heard God whisper her name; therefore, she knows that He still moves stones. She is the gentle thunder who knows that the angels are never silent.

Priscilla is more than a conqueror. Indeed, she is more than just the straw that stirs the shake—she is the flavor of the shake. Honey, may God forever smile favorably upon you, upon yours and upon all of your efforts!

TABLE OF CONTENTS

Introduction 9
Chapter One: **What Is Prayer?** 13
Chapter Two: **Precautions of Prayer** 23
Chapter Three: **Elements of Prayer** 31
Chapter Four: **Provisions of Prayer** 41
Chapter Five: **Aerobics of Prayer** 51
Chapter Six: **Praying Scripture** 59
Chapter Seven: **Utilizing a Prayer Model** 73
Chapter Eight: **Ways God Answers Prayer** 79
Chapter Nine: **Why God Delays Answering Prayer** 87
Chapter Ten: **What God Does When I Pray** 95
Chapter Eleven: **What Does Prayer Do?** 101
Chapter Twelve: **Intercessory Prayers** 109
Chapter Thirteen: **Pray Before Deciding** 119
Chapter Fourteen: **Praying in the Spirit** 127
Chapter Fifteen: **Praying Through Your Addictions** 139
Epilogue 149

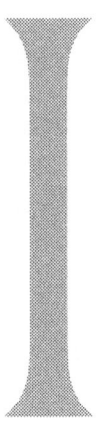 # INTRODUCTION

Introduction

Have you ever wondered why your prayers aren't answered?

Have you ever wondered if God listens to you when you pray?

Are you about ready to give up on prayer all together because it seems so futile?

If this is you, then this book is for you. The fact is that God may not be answering your prayers. However, the truth is that God answers prayer. Maybe there's something that needs to be corrected in your prayer life. Maybe there is something you're unaware of that needs attention.

God, Listen! will guide you through the wilderness of unanswered prayer to the Promised Land of communion with God. If you're ready to leave Egypt behind and to set your face toward Canaan, then this book is for you.

With **God, Listen!** you'll be able to:

- Take charge of your prayer life and begin to pray prayers that avail much.

- Capture the heart of God as you present your petitions to Him.

- Stop the enemy in his tracks as you prayerfully consider each situation and decision you are faced with.

- Live in the bounty promised by the Heavenly Father.

The words that moved St. Augustine to read the letter to the Romans were those of a child: Take. Read. Those same words are resonating now. Unlock the door to answered prayer. Take. Read.

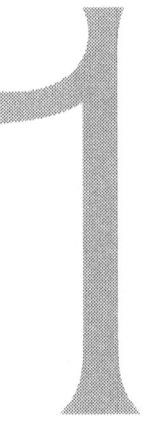

CHAPTER ONE

WHAT IS PRAYER?

1 What Is Prayer?

It happened that while Jesus was praying in a certain place, after He had finished, one of His disciples said to Him, Lord, teach us to pray just as John also taught his disciples.

And He said to them, "When you pray, say: Father, hallowed be Your name. Your kingdom come.

(Luke 11:1,2)

Jesus prayed often and long. Prayer, for Him, wasn't an elective but an essential element for developing spiritual stamina. On one occasion after praying, Jesus disciples asked Him to teach them how to pray, so He did.

This demonstrates that prayer is both teachable and learnable. It's not just a spontaneous, random mumbling of meaningless words.

Do you receive more requests for singing or for prayer? Very likely, prayer is your most frequently solicited spiritual service. Therefore, because others depend on your prayers, you ought to learn how to pray effectively.

Verbalizing Faith

Jesus taught his disciples to say one particular thing when they prayed, ...*When you pray, say: Father...* (Luke 11:2). Prayer is directed to your Heavenly Father, and is a verbalization of your faith. Prayer verbalizes your perception of the actions and/or desired actions of Almighty God.

Jesus Christ provides access to the Heavenly Father. He is the mediating High Priest. *Therefore, since we have a great high priest who has passed through the heavens, Jesus the Son of God, let us hold fast our confession* (Heb. 4:14).

He is the only mediator, *For there is one God, and one mediator also between God and men,*

> **Prayer is a verbalization of your faith.**

the man Christ Jesus (1 Tim. 2:5). Through Him you can draw near to God with confidence (Heb. 4:16). Therefore, only Jesus can provide access for your prayers to the Heavenly Father.

Some believe that praying the rosary and inviting Mary, the mother of Jesus, to pray offers advantages. However, Scripture doesn't teach that Mary ever had any intercessory power above that of any other individual. The Bible teaches that Jesus is the one mediator between God and men, not His mother.

Therefore, I believe that to pray the rosary is to do violence to the teachings of Scripture. To pray the rosary is to ask Mary to do what only Jesus can do.

When you pray, you are not only verbalizing your faith to the Father through Jesus Christ, but doing so with the Holy Spirit's help. The Holy Spirit facilitates prayer on your behalf, ...*the Spirit Himself intercedes for us* (Rom. 8:26). To intercede is to rescue.

Suppose that you received limited information about an automobile accident involving a very dear friend. The tragedy overwhelms you, and so you're unable to collect your thoughts to pray. Don't worry. The Holy Spirit intercedes for you.

When you collect your thoughts, what would you pray for since you have only limited information? You may pray for total and complete recovery. But what if your friend has already expired? Don't worry. The Holy Spirit intercedes for you; He rescues you.

During times of weakness, the Holy Spirit rescues you from your own ignorance of how to pray as you ought. However, these times of weakness should be the exception and not the rule for your prayer life.

Visualizing Faith

Prayer is not just what you say, but is what you say that you've seen through faith. Not only is prayer a verbalization, but it's also a visualization of your faith. Before you can verbalize your faith, you must first visualize your faith. Therefore prayer is also a visualization of your faith.

> **Prayer is a visualization of your faith.**

Before you can pray for something, you must first see it. When someone asks for directions to your house, you visualize the route first before you answer. Before you can open your mouth and speak something, you must see something. Mental pictures precede verbal pronouncements. You may not always be able to say what you see, but you can never say what you cannot see.

What should you visualize? Visualize a Heavenly Father who listens to your prayers. The inability to visualize God listening makes praying extremely difficult. Have you ever been talking to someone on the telephone and suddenly heard a dial tone? What did you do? You probably verified that someone was listening before continuing your conversation.

Divine Communication

How you see yourself and God dictates your prayer life, because prayer is two-way communication with God. Those who have learned to pray have learned to commune with God.

God does listen. In fact, God is always listening. Visualize Him listening to you and keep talking. God relates to humanity and to the world. But God doesn't just listen, He also responds. Contentment reigns when you can visualize God listening. But frustration rules when you're unsure if God is listening.

During the days of Elijah, worshippers called on their god, Baal. They cried out to him from morning to noon, yet Baal never answered.

Then they took the ox which was given them and they prepared it and called on the name of Baal from morning until noon saying, O Baal, answer us. But there was no voice and no one answered. And they leaped about the altar which they made (1 Kings 18:26).

They imagined that Baal was listening to respond, but he never did. Their futility and frustration even drove them to mutilate their bodies (1 Kings 18:28).

Thank God for Jesus Christ! God always listens to the voice of the righteous, ...*And His ears attend to their prayer* (1 Peter 3:12). If God isn't listening to you, it's your own fault. You can demand an audience with God. What wonderful assurance!

Visualize Jesus providing priority access for you to talk to your Father. The Bible declares that incense was used to help believers visualize their prayers rising toward heaven, ...*golden bowls full of incense, which are the prayers of the saints* (Rev. 5:8). Obviously, visualization enhanced their spiritual perspective (Rev. 8:3-4). You too should visualize the Holy Spirit assisting as Jesus grants authority for you to talk to your Heavenly Father.

You ought to learn to pray! Yes, see and say! Why say? Saying reinforces what you see. Thoroughly visualize before you verbalize in prayer.

Thought-provoking Questions

1. How does concentrating on your verbalization of faith enhance your prayer life?

2. How does concentrating on your visualization of faith enhance your prayer life?

3. How can you ensure a healthy balance between verbalizing and visualizing of faith in prayer?

CHAPTER TWO

PRECAUTIONS FOR PRAYER

Precautions for Prayer

When you pray, you are not to be like the hypocrites; for they love to stand and pray in the synagogues and on the street corners so that they may be seen by men. Truly I say to you, they have their reward in full.

But you, when you pray, go into your inner room, close your door and pray to your Father who is in secret, and your Father who sees what is done in secret will reward you.

(Matt. 6:5-6)

Many have incorrectly called the prayer recorded in Matthew 6:5-15, the Lord's Prayer. This is not it, but there is a Lord's Prayer recorded in Scripture. Its in John:

Jesus spoke these things; and lifting up His eyes to heaven, He said, Father, the hour has come; glorify Your Son, that the Son may glorify You. . . . .and I have made Your name known to them, and will make it known, so that the love with which You loved Me may be in them, and I in them.
(John 17:1, 26)

Model Prayer

Jesus could never have prayed the prayer recorded in Matthew 6 for Himself, because He owed no debts: *And forgive us our debts, as we also have forgiven our debtors* (Matt. 6:12). Rather, He told the disciples this is how they should pray (Matt. 6:9).

> **Public prayers should be understandable to those listening.**

The disciples were not to just pray the words of this prayer; it's the manner in which they should pray. Jesus didn't teach them what they should pray, but how they should pray. This prayer only served as a model for His disciples. Yes, using this model prayer Jesus taught His disciples to pray. Likewise, by observing this model prayer, you may also learn to pray.

Jesus encountered some hypocrites who prayed ineffective prayers. The word hypocrite came from the Greek word *hypo krino*. *Hypo* meant *under* while *krino* meant *to judge*.

Our idea of play actor comes from this word. An actor assumes the identity of another person and then projects himself as if he were that individual. Hence, hypocrites hid their true identities and assumed the identities of others. These hypocrites behaved as religious play actors. They dressed up in a prayer life, assumed the identity of the people of God though they themselves resided within the domain of Satan.

Ineffective Prayer

These hypocrites prayed ineffective prayers and hosted an invalid purpose for praying. They prayed to be seen of men,

> *When you pray, you are not to be like the hypocrites; for they love to stand and pray in the synagogues and on the street corners so that they may be seen by men. Truly I say to you, they have their reward in full.*
>
> (Matt. 6:5)

They stood in the synagogues and on the corners for increased visibility. Interestingly, they reached their goal and achieved their reward, "they have their reward in full."

Jesus never opposed standing to pray but He did oppose standing to be seen (Luke 18:9-14). Nor did Jesus prohibit praying publicly. The Scriptures encourage you to pray publicly.

The apostle Paul insisted that public prayers be understandable to those listening (1 Cor. 14:13-26). Seemingly, these hypocrites prayed publicly what should have been prayed privately (Matt. 6:6; 21:13).

Jesus also encountered some Gentiles who prayed ineffective prayers. In this context, the Gentiles were those who were unconnected with the people of God.

Invalid Prayer

These Gentiles prayed ineffective prayers because they followed an invalid procedure for praying. They used meaningless repetition, *And when you are praying, do not use meaningless repetition as the Gentiles do, for they suppose that they will be heard for their many words* (Matt. 6:7). Meaningless repetitions weren't meaningless simply because they repeated them. They were meaningless because they were void of spiritual substance. These Gentiles thought that God would hear them because of the quantity of their words, rather than the quality of their words.

Jesus never prohibited repetition within prayer, and He never prohibited repeating the same prayer. He even repeated Himself in prayer, *And He (Jesus) left them again, and went away and prayed a third time, saying the same thing once more* (Matt. 26:44). Jesus opposed not the repetition of prayer but the repetition of the insignificance of their prayer.

Always ask yourself these questions:

- Why am I praying?

- How am I praying?

- Is my prayer consistent with the prayer principles I have learned from the word of God?

Your prayers say something about your characterization of God. Historically. the people of God prayed as they characterized Him. Hezekiah and David requested the divine intervention of God in accordance with how they characterized His sovereignty (2 Kings 19:15-19; 1 Chron. 29:10-19).

> **Your prayers say something about your characterization of God.**

Honor the precautions. But, state your true concerns and feelings to God. Complain of Him, to Him, but remember to praise Him as well. Go ahead and question your faith in Him. Bargain with Him if you like. Try to influence Him to do what you think is best. He understands.

Thought-provoking Questions

1. How different should your public prayers be from your private prayers?

2. How does your characterization of God affect your complaints and praise to God?

3. To what extent should you complain about God, and when does it irritate Him?

CHAPTER THREE
Elements of Prayer

3 ELEMENTS OF PRAYER

Pray, then, in this way: Our Father who is in heaven, Hallowed be Your name. Your kingdom come. Your will be done, on earth as it is in heaven.

(Matt. 6:9-10)

Destination

Jesus taught His disciples that the Father in Heaven was the destination of their prayer, *Pray, then in this way: Our Father who is in Heaven* (Matt. 6:9). What did Jesus mean? He meant for them to acknowledge **that** God is in heaven and to acknowledge **the** God who is in heaven. He wanted them to recognize that God is sovereign to every earthly being and entity. Therefore, address your prayers only to **the** God who is **in** heaven.

We should never reduce God to just some mystical force. The once popular, Arsenio Hall, regularly referred to the "god force" within you. God is more than just a god or good force. Others have even referred to God as just the god of the best of your understanding. For some the god of the best of their understanding is not the God of heaven. They are those, *whose end is destruction, whose god is their appetite, and whose glory is in their shame, who set their minds on earthly things* (Phil. 3:19).

Acknowledging God as your Father implies that you've been born again as His child. The Father disciplines His children (Heb. 12:5-10), and only those who submit to the discipline of the Father can expect to enjoy the privileges of being a child. Never do as some who say, I want everything that my Father gives, but I detest his discipline. Children love their earthly parents as long as they are receiving children's benefits. However, when parents exercise parental discipline, children no longer want to be children.

> **God is more than just a god or good force.**

Adoration

Jesus taught His disciples that the name of the Father was hallowed, *Pray, then, in this way: 'Our Father who is in heaven, hallowed be Your name* (Matt. 6:9). What did Jesus mean? He meant to always acknowledge the name of the Father.

The apostles, Peter and John, healed a lame man, and the authorities demanded to know by what power or in what name they had done so. Peter and John credited the power to the name of Jesus (Acts 4:7-12). To acknowledge the name of the Father implies that you recognize His authority, character, and/or reputation.

Acknowledging that the name of the Father is hallowed honors His holiness. The word *hallowed* comes from the same root word as the words *holy* and *sanctified*. To make something hallowed, holy or sanctified, is to set it apart for a particular purpose. Therefore, set apart the name of God Almighty for only the distinct purpose that He approves.

The Father is prominent yet personal, so never reduce God to being just an errand boy. When you run out of something, do you expect God to run and get it for you?

Acknowledge God's name as hallowed by submitting to His authority, imitating His character, and upholding His character. The apostle Paul charged some folk with blaspheming the name of God for failing to submit to His authority, imitate His character and uphold His character, *For the name of God is blasphemed among the Gentiles because of you, just as it is written* (Rom. 2:24). The essence of prayer, then, becomes more than what you say, it becomes your manner of living, so live according to your prayer.

If you provide your children with clean and neatly ironed clothes to wear, but they dress in dirty, ragged, and wrinkled clothing, how would you feel? What would others think? More than likely, you would feel embarrassed and disappointed and others would think that you are a negligent parent.

When you live a life void of the blessings that God provides, His name is dishonored. You blaspheme the name of God, not just by angrily using it as a swear word, but by failing to honor the challenge to live a life of consecration. Prayer then becomes more than just a way of speaking—it becomes a way of living (Mark 7:6-7).

Expectation

Jesus taught His disciples to expect the kingdom to come, *Pray, then in this way...Your kingdom come* (Matt. 6:9-10). What did Jesus mean? The prophets prophesied that a kingdom would come (Isaiah 9:6-7; Dan. 2:36-44). The preachers preached that a kingdom would come (Matt. 3:1-2; 4:17-23). Yet, the kingdom delayed in coming. Therefore, Jesus taught the disciples to pray for what they expected to come.

Thank God the kingdom has now come! The apostle Paul was in the kingdom and he declared, *For He rescued us from the domain of darkness, and transferred us to the kingdom of His beloved Son* (Col. 1:13). You need not pray a prayer of expectation for that which already is. Therefore, you need not pray for the kingdom to come. If you were praying for someone to arrive safely, what would you pray for after they had arrived safely? You would pray a prayer of thanksgiving for their safe arrival, not one of expectation for them to arrive.

Acceptance

Jesus taught the disciples to accept the will of the Father, *Your will be done, on earth as it is in heaven* (Matt. 6:10). What did Jesus mean? The children of the Father exercise their privileges and ask, but they must ultimately surrender to the will and final authority of the Father. Regardless of human preferences, the will of the Father exercises its final authority.

> **Regardless of human preferences, the will of the Father exercises its final authority.**

With God, there exists an ideal will, which is the ultimate maximum of His preference. Sinless perfection is the ideal will of God, *My little children, I am writing these things to you so that you may not sin* (1 John 2:1a). Husbands and wives remaining married honors the ideal will of God, *But to the married I give instructions, not I, but the Lord, that the wife should not leave her husband* (1 Cor. 7:10).

With God, there also exists a circumstantial will that answers the question, If we fail to achieve the ideal will, what now? Reconciliation is the circumstantial will of God, *(but if she does leave, she must remain unmarried, or else be reconciled to her husband), and that the husband should not divorce his wife* (1 Cor. 7:11). Confession is the circumstantial will of God, *If we confess our sins, He is faithful and righteous to forgive us our sins and to cleanse us from all unrighteousness* (1 John 1:9).

With God, there also exists a permissive will, which answers the question, What will God allow or permit? The apostle Paul demonstrated this well. Paul had spent time in Ephesus, so prior to setting sail for Caesarea, he expressed his desire to return there later. He didn't know whether God would permit him to, so he prayed in this manner, *I will return to you again if God wills* (Acts 18:21). God would decide whether Paul would ever return to this mission field or come home to be with Him.

Paul also acknowledged the permissive will of God in his desire to go to Rome, *But I will come to you soon, if the Lord wills* (1 Cor. 4:19a). Heretofore, his desire to visit Rome had remained unsatisfied (Rom. 1:13). Paul honored what Jesus had taught His disciples, that prayer needed the final approval of God.

James acknowledged uncertainties regarding things about which God has not definitively spoken (James 4:13-15). For these uncertainties, you should say, If God wills. However, you shouldn't say, "If it is Your will" regarding things about which God has already expressed His will. For these you should pray with full assurance (James 1:5-7). You know that it's the will of God for everyone to know truth (1 Tim. 2:1-4), so never pray, If it be Your will for one to know truth.

Thought-provoking Questions

1. How does God discipline us, directly or indirectly? By what He causes? By what He allows?

2. To what extent will God grant children's privileges to those who fail to submit to the Father's discipline?

3. How does the ideal, circumstantial and permissive will of God relate to each other?

CHAPTER TWO

Provisions in Prayer

4 PROVISIONS IN PRAYER

So do not be like them; for your Father knows what you need before you ask Him. Pray, then, in this way:

Our Father who is in heaven, Hallowed be Your name. Your kingdom come. Your will be done, On earth as it is in heaven. Give us this day our daily bread. And forgive us our debts, as we also have forgiven our debtors. And do not lead us into temptation, but deliver us from evil. For Yours is the kingdom and the power and the glory forever. Amen.

For if you forgive others for their transgressions, your heavenly Father will also forgive you. But if you do not forgive others, then your Father will not forgive your transgressions.

(Matt. 6:8-15)

Jesus informed His disciples that God knew what they needed even before they asked, *So do not be like them; for your Father knows what you need before you ask Him* (Matt. 6:8). Yet, He taught them to ask God to supply their needs.

Physical and Tangible Nutrients

Jesus taught His disciples to ask God to supply their physical and tangible nutrition, by teaching them to ask for bread: *Give us this day our daily bread* (Matt. 6:11). Bread symbolized the supply and provision for everything they needed for their bodily growth and development. It sustained them physically.

Bread contains the necessary physical nourishments needed to sustain human life. Without it, nothing else really matters. Esau attested to this fact. He was so famished on one occasion that he sold his birthright for a meal (Gen. 25:29-34). Likewise, hunger pains

> **Jesus taught His disciples to ask God to supply their physical and tangible nutrition.**

shocked the prodigal son into repentance and sent him scurrying home (Luke 15:14-18).

When Jesus taught His disciples to ask the Heavenly Father for bread, it's very possible that they thought of the forty-year feast of manna that God provided for the children of Israel during their trek through the wilderness (Exodus 16:35). Except for the Sabbath day, God provided only enough manna to supply the daily needs of the Israelites:

> *Then the Lord said to Moses, Behold, I will rain bread from heaven for you; and the people shall go out and gather a day's portion every day, that I may test them, whether or not they will walk in My instruction. On the sixth day, when they prepare what they bring in, it will be twice as much as they gather daily.*
> *(Exodus 16:4-5)*

Jesus taught the disciples to ask for their daily bread. God used this principle to teach the Israelites to depend daily upon God, and Jesus used it to teach the disciples the same thing. By doing so, they would never fall into the pride of self-sufficiency.

This prayer indicates how specific God wants His people to pray not only for **what** they want but **when** they want it: *Give us this day...* (Matt. 6:11). Indeed, God exercises compassionate concern for His children.

Include in your daily prayers specific requests for your bodily needs. You may think it's wrong to pray for such trivia, but if it's wrong to pray for such, then it would be wrong to desire to obtain it. Likewise, you may be embarrassed to talk to God about such trivial needs. If that's so, then why aren't you embarrassed to desire such trivial needs?

Protection

Jesus taught His disciples to pray for their spiritual and intangible nutrition by teaching them to ask for forgiveness: *And forgive us our debts, as we also have forgiven our debtors* (Matt. 6:12). Forgiveness is a basic need for spirituality. Without forgiveness, no person can ever stand in the Holy presence of God.

Forgiveness is a cancellation of debts. Long ago God engraved debt cancellation into the hearts of his people. Using the Sabbath Year, which was a year of debt release, God taught His people about forgiveness:

> *At the end of every seven years you shall grant a remission of debts. This is the manner of remission: every creditor shall release what he has loaned to his neighbor; he shall not exact it of his neighbor and his brother, because the Lord's remission has been proclaimed.*
>
> (Deuteronomy 15:1-2)

God also used the Year of Jubilee, every 50th year, to further teach His people about forgiving debts. Every 50th year the people released their slaves and returned their lands to the original families to whom it was given during the initial division of the Promised Land (Leviticus 25:8-13, 23-28).

Forgiveness is consistent with the character of God and contingent upon the character of man. Those who receive forgiveness must be willing to give forgiveness. If you are unwilling to forgive others, God is unwilling to forgive you, *But if you do not forgive others, then your Father will not forgive your transgressions* (Matt. 6:15).

> **Jesus taught His disciples to pray for their spiritual and intangible nutrition.**

Jesus emphasized this reciprocal responsibility when He told the story of a slave who owed the king $1,000,000 but was unable to pay the debt. At first, the king was going to pursue legal proceedings and drag him to court. However, the slave begged for an extension of the credit term and the king mercifully forgave the entire debt.

Shortly, thereafter, the same slave confronted a fellow slave who owed him $2. This fellow slave begged for an extension of the credit term, but received no mercy. When word of what happened reached the king, he reversed his earlier decision and handed his slave over to, Bruiser, the enforcer (Matt. 18:21-35).

Directions

Jesus also taught His disciples to pray for their spiritual direction, *And do not lead us into temptation, but deliver us from evil. For Yours is the kingdom and the power and the glory forever. Amen* (Matt. 6:13). What did He mean?

Jesus taught the disciples to ask God to lead them in a direction of avoidance. Temptations were trials of experience that tested them, proving their character. This test informed them of their character, not God. Nevertheless, they could ask God to lead them so they wouldn't need to undergo those trials of experience (Heb. 5:5-11).

Jesus taught the disciples to ask God to lead them in the direction of endurance. To deliver from evil, is to rescue from the evil one. They could ask God to lead them so they wouldn't encounter Satan himself.

Thought-provoking Questions

1. Why should you ask God when He already knows what you need?

2. How specific should you be in asking for your everyday necessities of life?

3. How does prayer contrast with human effort?

CHAPTER FIVE

AEROBICS OF PRAYER

5

AEROBICS OF PRAYER

Therefore let one who speaks in a tongue pray that he may interpret. For if I pray in a tongue, my spirit prays, but my mind is unfruitful. What is the outcome then? I will pray with the spirit and I will pray with the mind also; I will sing with the spirit and I will sing with the mind also. Otherwise if you bless in the spirit only, how will the one who fills the place of the ungifted say the Amen at your giving of thanks, since he does not know what you are saying? For you are giving thanks well enough, but the other person is not edified.

(1 Cor. 14:13-17)

Occasionally, the Corinthians prayed in tongues. A tongue was a language foreign to those who prayed, so a prayer prayed in a tongue needed to be interpreted: *Therefore let one who speaks in a tongue pray that he may interpret. For if I pray in a tongue, my spirit prays, but my mind is unfruitful* (1 Cor. 14:13-14). Without an interpretation, those who prayed in a tongue wouldn't understand their own prayer.

Pray With Your Mind

Those who prayed in a tongue prayed with only their spirit and not with their mind. When they prayed with only their spirit, their mind benefited nothing from the prayer experience (1 Cor. 14:13-17). God encouraged them to pray also with their mind (1 Cor. 14:15).

In addition to benefiting your spirit, your prayers should engage your mind. Your mind should be exercised when you pray for forgiveness, because you must understand how prayer contributes to forgiveness.

> **Prayer alone never produces strength.**

Prayer alone never produces forgiveness. Only by producing repentance can prayer produce forgiveness (Acts

2:38; 8:20-22). Moreover, it's only to the extent that prayer causes repentance that prayer can secure forgiveness. Therefore, you need to pray for repentance, or at least understand that repentance is a necessary step towards obtaining forgiveness.

Your prayers should exercise your mind when you pray for strength. You must understand how prayers contribute to strength.

Prayer alone never produces strength. Only by producing digestion of the Word (the food of God) and exercise of spiritual gifts can prayer produce strength (1 Peter 2:1-2; Colossians 1:9-11; Eph. 3:16). Only to the extent that prayer causes digestion and exercise can prayer produce strength.

Therefore, you must pray for digestion of the food of God and appropriate spiritual exercise. At least you must understand how that digestion and exercise are necessary steps toward obtaining strength.

Have you asked for prayer for strength and then passed up the very next Bible study session? Have you asked for prayer and then refused to engage in the next spiritual exercise? If so, you will never gain strength. You've wasted your time asking and the time of those who prayed.

Hear With Your Mind

Praying in tongues engages only the spirit of the one who prays, not the mind of those who hear. Saints assemble for edification, so the apostle Paul discouraged praying in tongues in the assembly unless an interpretation came forth. While discouraging praying in tongues, he encouraged praying for understanding. Those who heard needed to understand.

Some may say, When I pray it's between God and me. Those who hear should have nothing to do with it. According to divine insistence those who pray in the assembly must pray so that those who hear can understand.

Why? Those who hear need to agree with those who speak,

> *Otherwise if you bless in the spirit only, how will the one who fills the place of the ungifted say the Amen at your giving of thanks, since he does not know what you are saying?*
>
> (1 Cor. 14:16)

The word amen literally means so let it be, surely and/or truly. Saying Amen announces that you believe what the speaker has said. Saying Amen indicates that you agree with the trustworthy truths of the speaker. But, how can you honestly say that the speaker spoke trustworthy truths when you failed to understand his speech?

How can you agree when you don't understand what he said?

Amen affirms truth. In the New Testament, only the Lord used it at the *beginning* of a sentence (Matt. 5:18; 26; 6:2; 16:28; Luke 9:27; John 1:51; 2 Cor. 1:20), because only He can affirm truth from the beginning. You can affirm truth only at the ending, after you have heard and understood.

> **Occasionally, prayer requires action on the part of the hearer.**

Not only should you pray so that others can agree but so that they can act as well. Occasionally, prayer requires action on the part of the hearer. Some have heard prayers for their own forgiveness, but didn't realize that they needed to repent first. Some have heard prayers for their own strength, but didn't realize they needed to first digest the food of God and exercise their spiritual gifts. It's important to know and understand how prayers contribute to forgiveness and strength.

You don't pray to the audience, but you carry them along in the understanding of your prayer. The hearer needs to understand the relationship between the prayer request and the answer to the prayer request. Prayer during the assembly should exercise the mind of both the speaker and the hearers.

Prayer Needs Help

Paul censored the believers in the church at Corinth for praying prayers which failed to edify the hearers, *For you are giving thanks well enough, but the other person is not edified* (1 Cor. 14:17). To edify is to promote growth in Christian wisdom. Wisdom is knowledge of how to recognize and regulate your relationship with God. Your publicly heard prayers should promote growth in the knowledge of how to recognize and regulate the hearer's relationship with God.

Prayer alone never promotes growth in Christian wisdom. Prayer just promotes the elements that promote the growth in Christian wisdom. For example, the key never starts a car it simply promotes the elements that start the car. The key connects the starter to the source of energy, the battery. Therefore, God expects you to pray for the promotion of those elements that promote growth in Christian wisdom (Matt. 9:37-38).

Thought-provoking Questions

1. What is the benefit of understanding prayer in your mind?

2. How does prayer promote strength and growth in Christian wisdom?

3. Why is it important to know how prayer promotes growth and strength?

Chapter Six
Pray Scripture

6 Pray Scripture

It happened that while Jesus was praying in a certain place, after He had finished, one of His disciples said to Him, Lord, teach us to pray just as John also taught his disciples. And He said to them, When you pray, say:

Father, hallowed be Your name. Your kingdom come. Give us each day our daily bread. And forgive us our sins, For we ourselves also forgive everyone who is indebted to us. And lead us not into temptation.

(Luke 11:1-4)

Who taught you how to pray? How did they teach you to pray? Very likely, you learned how to pray by listening to others—your parents, siblings, and people at church. From what you heard you cut out a pattern for yourself and began to follow it.

What happens when you constantly hear prayers that are without spiritual substance? You learn to pray prayers that are void of spiritual substance.

Prayer may be your most frequently requested spiritual service as people ask you to pray for them. Therefore, you ought to learn how to pray. How strong is your desire to know how to pray?

Jesus taught his disciples to pray. In addition to using His model prayer, He modeled prayer for them (Matt. 6:1-15; Luke 11:1-4).

> **You, too, can fill your prayers with spiritual substance.**

The model prayer taught the disciples to exalt the name of the Heavenly Father and to expect both His tangible and intangible nurture. By listening, Jesus' disciples learned to exalt the name and expect the nurture of their Heavenly Father, and learned to fill their prayers with spiritual substance.

You, too, can fill your prayers with spiritual substance. God provides many models for prayer in Scripture, have you ever considered using them as your prayer model? Look in the Scriptures.

Study the prayer models, and learn how to fill your prayers with spiritual substance.

Holy Spirit-led Prayer Models

Locate in Scriptures the prayer of a Holy Spirit-led person—the apostle Paul for example. You'll find in the latter part of Ephesians chapter 1 the essence of a prayer that Paul prayed as the Holy Spirit led him. Notice how Paul exalted the name of the Father:

> *For this reason I too, having heard of the faith in the Lord Jesus which exists among you and your love for all the saints, do not cease giving thanks for you, while making mention of you in my prayers; that the God of our Lord Jesus Christ, the Father of glory, may give to you a spirit of wisdom and of revelation in the knowledge of Him. I pray that the eyes of your heart may be enlightened, so that you will know what is the hope of His calling, what are the riches of the glory of His inheritance in the saints.*
> (Eph. 1:15-18)

Paul expected the nurture of God. He prayed for illumination for the saints, and wanted their illumination to include a spirit of wisdom, knowledge of God, and enlightenment of heart. He also prayed for one thing so that something else could occur, *so that you will know* (Eph. 1:18).

Praying Scripture is different from just quoting Scripture. Praying Scripture extracts the elements of a previously prayed prayer and packages them in the present situation of the person who prays.

Suppose you decide to use this technique as you pray that a new believer will become more spiritually stable. Consider this example:

> *Dear God, the Father of our Lord Jesus Christ. Jimmy needs wisdom and understanding of how to lead his family. Grant him Your wisdom in abundance that he may know You and help his family to know You. Cause him to recognize Your calling, and help him experience the joy of his salvation.*

Locate in Scripture a prayer that a Holy Spirit-led person prayed and fashion your prayer according to the model. Consider how it exalted the name of God and expected His nurture.

By doing this, you'll never again pray prayers devoid of spiritual substance. Never again will you adopt terminology that

> **Praying Scripture is different from just quoting Scripture.**

is foreign to your understanding and wonder if it meets God's approval. Furthermore, you'll know that God approves of all your prayers. You can write your prayer, meditate on it and expand it to include other specifics, because spiritual variety will abound in all your prayers.

A Model for Thanksgiving

Herein lies a prayer of thanksgiving:

We give thanks to God always for all of you, making mention of you in our prayers; constantly bearing in mind your work of faith and labor of love and steadfastness of hope in our Lord Jesus Christ in the presence of our God and Father.
(1 Thess. 1:2-3)

This prayer provides an excellent model for prayer. With this prayer, Paul thanked God for what He had specifically done and would do.

How often do you fill your prayers with thanksgiving for someone else? Are you in the habit of filling your prayers with thanksgiving for the spiritual progression that you've seen in the lives of others? Or do you often complain about their lack of spiritual progression? Why not appreciate their growth and pray for more? Thank God for His work of faith expressed in the lives of other believers.

Paul remembered the difficulties of the Thessalonians and thanked God for their accomplishments. The believers in Thessalonica had become imitators of the men of God and had themselves become examples (1 Thess. 1:6-7). Their faith resounded throughout the region, and their reputation preceded even the travels of the apostle Paul (1 Thess. 1:8-10).

Do you count your blessings as you remember that God enables you because others are praying for you? The active faith of many others has blessed you abundantly, so you should reciprocate. How often do you thank God for keeping the conviction strong and hope alive in other believers? How long has it been since you prayed a prayer of thanks for their labor of love and work of faith?

Following this model will fill your prayers with spiritual substance. Pattern you prayers after principles within Scripture. Set aside one day per week to pray only prayers of thanksgiving. It will do your life good. Don't follow the selfish route of children, bringing only your requests but rarely expressing thanksgiving.

Requests

Though God already knows what you need, He wants you to ask Him to satisfy those needs, *but in everything by prayer and supplication with thanksgiving let your requests be made known to God* (Phil. 4:6). Therefore, God provides a model for prayer requests. The apostle Paul prayed for the opportunity to once again see believers face to face so that he could invest in their faith (1 Thess. 3:10-11). He wanted to ensure their faith become whole and remained healthy.

How long has it been since you prayed for the opportunity to visit and invest in the faith of another? Though this is a prayer of request, it snatches you out of your selfish zone and plants you in the midst of spiritual altruism. Likewise, Paul wanted the believers to invest in each other:

> *...and may the Lord cause you to increase and abound in love for one another, and for all people, just as we also do for you; so that He may establish your hearts without blame in holiness before our God and Father at the coming of our Lord Jesus with all His saints.*
>
> (1 Thess. 3:12-13)

Paul very pointedly called for love, the core of Christianity, to come forth. According to Jesus, love is the believers identification badge (John 13:34-35). Love for one another produces fertile hearts for God to perform His work, so Paul wanted these folk to love one another so that God could establish their hearts throughout all eternity. Paul frequently prayed for one thing so that something in addition would occur (2 Cor. 13:7-9).

How long has it been since you prayed that God would increase love in the hearts of believers? The answer to this prayer of request propels the church into eternity, basking in the glory of God.

The apostle Paul also prayed for the spiritual standing of believers: *To this end also we pray for you always, that our God will count you worthy of your calling, and fulfill every desire for goodness and the work of faith with power* (2 Thess. 1:11). The Greek word for *worthy*, means equal in weight. Paul prayed that God would consider them to be equal in weight with their calling, which was God's investment in them.

Once again, Paul prayed for one thing so that something in addition might occur. God called them so that they would fulfill His every desire. When they fulfill God's desire, He is glorified (2 Thess. 1:12). Therefore, we must not only pray that God makes an investment, but that those who receive His investment will in turn invest in God.

Ask Specifically for What You Want

How long has it been since you've asked someone to pray for you? Did you tell them what you wanted them to pray for? If not, how did they know for what to pray? I don't believe that Scripture records a time when the apostles or prophets asked for prayer and failed to state specifically what they wanted.

Paul requested a specific prayer:

> *Finally, brethren, pray for us that the word of the Lord will spread rapidly and be glorified, just as it did also with you; and that we will be rescued from perverse and evil men; for not all have faith.*
>
> (2 Thess. 3:1-2)

Paul desired hindrance-free missionary opportunities. First, he wanted receptive hearts in those who would hear. Second, he wanted to be removed from those unbelievers who refused to hear. Today, you may pray that prayer like this: *Lord lead me away from those who just want to argue and lead me to people who are interested to obey.*

Paul prayed for effective evangelism among others just as he had experienced with those of Thessalonica (1 Thess. 2:13-14). Lack of prayer impedes the free course of the Word of God.

Answered Prayer Models

Peter and John were going into the temple to pray when they met a lame man. When he cried out for some money, they proceeded to heal him. This man jumped up and praised God, shouting and leaping for joy.

The Jewish officials interrogated Peter and John, and commanded them to speak no more about the resurrection of Jesus and the power of His name. When they refused to be silent, the officials became fearful because of their glorifying of God.

Upon being released, Peter and John assembled with other believers. There they lifted their voices in one accord and prayed to God, exalting His name. They referenced his authority, saying:

> *O Lord, it is You who made the heaven and the earth and the sea, and all that is in them, who by the Holy Spirit, through the mouth of our father David Your servant, said,*
>
> *Why did the gentiles rage, and the peoples devise futile things? The kings of the earth took their stand, and the rulers were gathered together against the LORD and against his Christ.*
>
> *For truly in this city there were gathered together against Your holy servant Jesus, whom You anointed, both Herod and Pontius Pilate, along with the Gentiles and the peoples of Israel, to do whatever Your hand and Your purpose predestined to occur.*
>
> (Acts 4:24-28)

Not only did they exalt the name of the Lord, they expected His nurture as well:

And now, Lord, take note of their threats, and grant that Your bond-servants may speak Your word with all confidence, while You extend Your hand to heal, and signs and wonders take place through the name of Your holy servant Jesus.
(Acts 4:29-30)

First they exalted His name and then requested His nurture. They requested the courage and confidence needed to speak boldly.

Guess what! God answered immediately, *And when they had prayed, the place where they had gathered together was shaken, and they were all filled with the Holy Spirit and began to speak the word of God with boldness* (Acts 4:31). They received the courage they requested.

Locate a prayer in Scripture that God answered and then fashion your prayer according to the model. Consider how it exalted the name of God and expected His nurture.

God wants you to utilize the prayer models that He has provided so that your spiritual substance will be evident. You don't have to remain deficient in your prayer life. As many models for prayer as there are in the Scriptures, you have no excuse.

Thought-provoking Questions

1. How did you learn to pray?

2. How can the prayers of Holy Spirit-led people help you?

3. How can the prayers of those who received an answer help you?

Chapter Seven

7 Develop Your Prayer After a Model

7 Develop Your Prayer After a Model

It happened that while Jesus was praying in a certain place, after He had finished, one of His disciples said to Him, Lord, teach us to pray just as John also taught his disciples. And He said to them, When you pray, say:

Father, hallowed be Your name. Your kingdom come. Give us each day our daily bread. And forgive us our sins, For we ourselves also forgive everyone who is indebted to us. And lead us not into temptation.

(Luke 11:1-4)

Since, you are going to pray, you ought to spend some time learning how to pray. Knowing that you know how to pray enriches your life.

You need a model for praying in accordance with the will of God. Look in the Scriptures and find a prayer that was prayed by a Holy Spirit-led person that God answered. Obviously, these prayers pleased God.

> **You need a model for praying in accordance with the will of God.**

Steps to Following Prayer Models

(1) Select a prayer model in Scripture that addresses your situation.

(2) Read that model until you conceptualize its essence.

(3) Visualize the Father readily listening to answer your prayer.

(4) Make a written note of the elements of that prayer.

(5) Note how the prayer exalts the name of the Father.

(6) Note the destination of the prayer

(7) Note the adoration of the prayer

(8) Note the expectations, the nurture of the Father.

(9) Note the acceptance of the prayer

(10) Personalize and customize the principles of these items so that they speak specifically to your situation.

(11) Incorporate your written note into the verbalization of your prayer.

You may think that by doing this the prayer will be somebody else's and not yours. However, its likely that you'll always be praying the prayers of another, just make sure it contains spiritual substance. When you follow the Scripture model, you will know that God sanctions your prayers for their spiritual substance.

> **Personalize those ideas and concepts in your prayer.**

Make note of the essence of fifty prayers. Then, anytime you pray you can pull out an appropriate model. This activity will add spiritual variety to your prayer life.

Ingredients

When you want to bake a cake, you follow a model or recipe (written or remembered) for the kind of cake you are baking. You don't pull out a recipe for cornbread if you want a cake, because if you did, you wouldn't get what you want. Instead, you pull out the model that will lead to your desired result. Likewise, before you pray, pull out a model prayer that will best lead to the desired results.

Read that model and locate specific principles that apply to the situation about which you are praying. Then, personalize those ideas and concepts in your prayer.

Thought-provoking Questions

1. How does writing your prayer help you conceptualize and improve your prayer life?

2. What are the essential ingredients in prayer?

3. How does following a prayer model affect the personaless and sincerity of the prayer?

CHAPTER EIGHT

HOW DOES GOD ANSWER PRAYER

How Does God Answer Prayer

Then He said to them, Suppose one of you has a friend, and goes to him at midnight and says to him, Friend, lend me three loaves for a friend of mine has come to me from a journey, and I have nothing to set before him;~and from inside he answers and says, Do not bother me; the door has already been shut and my children and I are in bed; I cannot get up and give you anything. I tell you, even though he will not get up and give him anything because he is his friend, yet because of his persistence he will get up and give him as much as he needs.

(Luke 11:5-8)

Inside the contextual environment of the model prayer, Jesus emphasized how persistence brings rewards when making a request of a friend (Luke 11:5-8). He told the story of a person who at midnight had a visitor, but no food for the visitor to eat. The foodless man went to a friend's house, knocked on the door and asked for food. His friend reminded him that he was in bed and could not get up and give food. But because of the persistence and shamelessness of the one asking, he would arise and give food to the hungry.

The Lord's Reputation

The Lords reputation is at stake. Public knowledge of His refusal to provide for His children would shame His name. Therefore, the Lord gives to protect His own reputation.

> **Therefore, the Lord gives to protect His own reputation.**

Within the same contextual environment, Jesus spoke another foundational truth about God (Luke 11:13). He argued that God would give the Holy Spirit to those who ask, proving that God responds to prayer.

God promised to respond to the prayers of His children. The model prayer of Jesus reflects this truth. The Our Father indicates that God recognizes those praying as His children. Those whom He recognizes as children should honor Him as Father.

The psalmist prayed and God answered. Indeed, the psalmist learned to believe that God responded to the prayers of His people, *The eyes of the Lord are toward the righteous and His ears are open to their cry* (Psalms 34:15). Quoting almost verbatim, the apostle Peter concurred with the psalmist, *For the Eyes of the Lord are toward the Righteous, and His ears attend to their prayer* (1 Peter 3:12).

The Lord's Response

God responds to the prayers of His children in four different ways. **First**. God may give you exactly what you ask for. Zacharias and Elizabeth prayed for a son, and the angel appeared and confirmed that God had heard their prayers. He also delivered the promise of the birth of their son (Luke 1:5-13).

When God gives you exactly what you ask for, it's easy to connect His response to your prayer. But, do you take time to thank God that He has answered your prayer? When you begin to pray prayers of thanksgiving, you'll always connect God's response to your requests.

Second. God may give you less than what you ask for. The great lawgiver, Moses, asked God for an opportunity to cross over the Jordan and see the land of Canaan. God denied the fullness of his request, but did lead him up on a mountain so that he could see the Promised Land across the Jordan (Deuteronomy 1:34, 3:23-26). God gave him less than he asked for.

When God gives you less than what you ask for, you must connect God's response to your request. Do you readily appreciate God when He gives you exactly what you ask for but reluctantly appreciate Him when He gives you less than what you ask for?

God decided not to allow Moses to enter the Promised Land:

> *But the Lord said to Moses and Aaron, "Because you have not believed Me, to treat Me as holy in the sight of the sons of Israel, therefore you shall not bring this assembly into the land which I have given them.*
> (Numbers 20:12)

> **God responds to the prayers of His children in four different ways.**

Later, when Moses pleaded with God for permission to enter, God didn't change His mind. The ban remained in place. However, leading Moses up the mountain to see the

Promised Land was God's answer of giving less than Moses asked. Moses needed to connect the answer from God to his prayer request.

Third. God may give you something other than what you ask for. The apostle Paul asked for the removal of a thorn in his flesh. God denied the request for its removal, but did give Paul grace and strength to endure (2 Cor. 12:7-9).

Flex Your Muscles

Your supervisor has stepped on your last nerve and you have prayed for relief in the work place. In answer to your prayers, God may not remove either you or your contentious supervisor. Instead, He may give you the spiritual stamina to endure. Opposition develops muscle.

When God gives you less than or other than what you ask, how do you respond? Do you behave like an immature child by poking out your lip and pouting?

How do you think Paul internalized God's answer to his request? Grace rather than removal of the thorn was indeed the divine answer. Therefore, Paul must connect God's answer to his request.

Fourth, (you are going to love this one). God may give more than you ask for. Solomon asked for an understanding heart to judge the people of God. Solomon's request touched God so powerfully that God gave him wisdom, prominence and riches like no other person had ever had (1 Kings 3:6-13).

When God gives you more than you ask, do you realize that it is indeed God's answer? How likely are you to overlook the graciousness of God?

How do you think King Solomon internalized God's answer to his request? Riches and rank in addition to wisdom became the order of the day for Solomon. If God had not told Solomon what He was granting, how quickly would Solomon have realized that his wealth was part of the answer to his prayer? You, too, need to recognize God's answers.

Pray with expectation, and associate God's answer to your prayer requests.

Thought-provoking Questions

1. What should you do when God doesn't answer your prayer the way you want Him to?

2. What should you do if God answers but you don't recognize His answer?

3. How different do you feel about God when He gives you less than what you ask, or something other than what you've asked?

CHAPTER NINE

WHY GOD DELAYS ANSWERING PRAYER

9

WHY GOD DELAYS ANSWERING PRAYER

These things I have written to you who believe in the name of the Son of God, so that you may know that you have eternal life. This is the confidence which we have before Him, that, if we ask anything according to His will, He hears us. And if we know that He hears us in whatever we ask, we know that we have the requests which we have asked from Him.

(1 John 5:13-15)

The Holy Spirit assures us that God will answer prayers that are consistent with His ideal, circumstantial and/or permissive will. God will answer your prayer. But why does He sometimes delay?

The Answer May Not Be Ready

The answer may yet be unprepared. You made a request of God and He has an answer for you, but the answer isn't yet ready. No, you didn't catch God off-guard, but there are times when you may ask for what is not yet prepared.

The Israelites prayed for deliverance from Egyptian bondage (Exodus 2:24) and God prepared Moses to deliver His answer (Exodus 3). However, God didn't deliver them immediately. Why? The answer, God's delivery process was yet unprepared.

Moses spent forty years in the wilderness, but God's answer wasn't even ready then. Moses returned to Egypt and negotiated with Pharaoh, but the answer was still not ready. Ten plagues afflicted the land, but the answer was not yet ready. Deliverance had not yet come. Why? The answer was not fully ready for them.

> The answer may yet be unprepared.

God is a God of timing, and He operates according to His timetable. He knows that some things must precede other things in order for you to fully experience the latter.

The disciples prayed for the Kingdom to come (Luke 11:1), so why was the Kingdom delayed in coming? The Holy Spirit had to come before the Kingdom could come (Acts 1:1-8).

The disciples prayed for the Holy Spirit to come (Luke 11:13), so why did God delay sending the Spirit? Jesus first had to die before the Spirit could come (John 16:7, 14:26).

The people prayed for a Savior to redeem them from the Law. Why the delay? Time had not come (John 7:6-8, Gal. 4:4).

When you are twenty-five you may pray for retirement, but you still must work for 30 years or become independently wealthy. However, in either case something must precede retirement.

Sometimes God delays the answer because the answer isn't ready for you. God may still be working out the details of your answer.

You Must Be Ready for the Answer

At other times, the answer is ready but you aren't. God delays your answer until you are ready for it. Otherwise, you may be unable to handle the answer.

The Israelites anticipated entering a land flowing with milk and honey. God wanted them to be there, but delayed delivering them. He realized it must be a consequential event. God promised the

Israelites that He would drive out the habitants of the land, so why didn't God just drive them out in one day and give the land to the Israelites? The Israelites weren't ready to handle the land:

> *I will send hornets ahead of you so that they will drive out the Hivites, the Canaanites, and the Hittites before you. I will not drive them out before you in a single year, that the land may not become desolate and the beasts of the field become too numerous for you. I will drive them out before you little by little, until you become fruitful and take possession of the land.*
>
> (Exodus 23:28-30)

God said He would answer their prayer, but not in one day, not in one week, not in one month, and not in one year. God delayed the answer because the Israelites weren't ready for the answer. They weren't ready to posses the land of Canaan.

> **Otherwise, you may be unable to handle the answer.**

Sometimes when you pray the answer isn't ready, so God has to work out the details. However, at other times, you aren't ready for the answer, so God must work out the details in you.

You may pray for forgiveness (Matt. 6:12), so why are you yet unforgiven (Matt. 6:14-15)?

You may pray for church growth, so why hasn't the church grown? Are you really ready for it? Are you prepared for the noise, the space requirements, the workers, etc.?

You may have prayed for a better job with more income? Are you really prepared for greater responsibility? Are you prepared to manage more income?

Thought-provoking Questions

1. How much does God deviate from His timetable in order to answer your prayers?

2. Why must God wait until His answer is ready for your?

3. Why must God wait until you are ready for His answer?

CHAPTER TEN

WHAT GOD DOES WHEN I PRAY

10 What God Does When I Pray

And now, Lord, take note of their threats, and grant that Your bond-servants may speak Your word with all confidence, while You extend Your hand to heal, and signs and wonders take place through the name of Your holy servant Jesus. And when they had prayed, the place where they had gathered together was shaken, and they were all filled with the Holy Spirit and began to speak the word of God with boldness.

(Acts 4:29-31)

When you pray, God does through you what you can do. Therefore, you participate in the answer to your prayers.

Expectations

When you pray you should always expect God to do something. Before you pray, God wants you to prepare to receive His answer.

Because of your prayer God gives you courage (Acts 4:29-31). He provided courage to speak in spite of the threats.

Also because of your prayer God gives you power (Acts 4:33). He provided the power to speak boldly in spite of the threats.

> Because of prayer God acts upon the elements for you.

God has given you the capacity to do certain things. He has enabled you to do whatever it is that you can do.

God will accomplish things through you. Those things that you can do, God will not do for you He will only do them through you. For example, through you, God will fill out a job application but He will not fill out the application for you.

Immediate and specific answer

The disciples prayed for courage to speak boldly. God spoke boldly through them, but not for them (Acts 4:28-33). When God does something through you, He energizes you, making it possible.

God provided the courage for the church to do what they could do by providing the power. When you pray, God does something now for you just as He did then for them. There are times that God does through you what you can do and then there are times God does for you what you cannot do.

Because of prayer God acts upon the elements for you (Acts 4:31). Without human effort, God just shook the elements of the place.

Because of prayer, God acts upon the hearts of other for you (Acts 4:32, 34, 37). God just influenced the hearts of the believers.

Jesus spoke a parable about prayer, emphasizing the value of persistent prayer (18:1). To not lose heart (faint) meant to not become desperate.

We must persist in prayer, because God will bring about justice for his elect (Luke 18:2-7). Our prayers don't bother God, nor is He worn out by our continually coming to Him. This parable of the judge emphasizes one quality of God, He will respond to His elect. The elect are those who have been chosen by the Lord (Mark 13:21-27) to remain faithful (1 Peter 1:10).

You must persist in prayer because God will bring about justice for his elect quickly (Luke 18:8). How quickly? Our time clock ticks faster when we are awaiting God's reward than when we are awaiting God's rebuke.

Nehemiah waited for four months (Chiselv was 3rd month in civil calendar and Nisan was the 7th month in civil calendar (Neh. 1:1-4; 2:1). The patriarchs of old waited centuries for fulfillment (Heb. 11:13).

For most people a three-minute response time for paramedics is quick. For the mother whose child has stopped breathing three minutes is an eternity.

Sometimes God is preparing the answer for you (Galatians 4:4), while at other times He's preparing you for the answer. In either case the answer delays. Nevertheless, divine giving awaits human asking: God does not impose His highest gift.

Thought-provoking Questions

1. Why does God withhold courage until you pray, and how does He provide it after you pray?

2. Why does God withhold power until you pray, and how does He provide it after you pray?

3. How long should you wait for God to answer before you seek another avenue for your answer?

CHAPTER ELEVEN

WHAT DOES PRAYER DO?

What Does Prayer Do?

When they had been released, they went to their own companions and reported all that the chief priests and the elders had said to them. And when they heard this, they lifted their voices to God with one accord and said, O Lord, it is You who made the heaven and the earth and the sea, and all that is in them, who by the Holy Spirit, through the mouth of our father David Your servant, said,

Why did the gentiles rage, and the peoples devise futile things? The kings of the earth took their stand, and the rulers were gathered together against the Lord and against his Christ.

For truly in this city there were gathered together against Your holy servant

Jesus, whom You anointed, both Herod and Pontius Pilate, along with the Gentiles and the peoples of Israel, to do whatever Your hand and Your purpose predestined to occur. And now, Lord, take note of their threats, and grant that Your bond-servants may speak Your word with all confidence, while You extend Your hand to heal, and signs and wonders take place through the name of Your holy servant Jesus. And when they had prayed, the place where they had gathered together was shaken, and they were all filled with the Holy Spirit and began to speak the word of God with boldness.

(Acts 4:23-31)

Jesus prayed often and long. He set aside time to pray and taught His disciples to pray. Jesus taught his disciples not to lose their confidence, *Men ought to always pray and not faint* (Luke 18:1). Jesus taught them that rather than lose heart, they were to pray. In spite of what happened they were to always pray.

> **Prayer brings you into a conscious awareness of God.**

You ought to pray often and long as well. Prayer should be a regular part of your spiritual experience. The more difficult life becomes the more time you ought to spend in prayer.

Prayer can be a stabilizing force in your life. When prayer becomes a stabilizing force in the core of your very spiritual life, you will not lose heart as often as you will when it is not.

Conscious Awareness

Prayer brings you into a conscious awareness of God. The apostle Paul addressed the spiritual service of the saints by reminding them of their need to pray with conscious awareness, and a mind of understanding (1 Cor. 14:15). Their conscious awareness of God became paramount in prayer.

Prayer brings you into a conscious awareness of the historical past. Prayer brought the early believers into a conscious awareness of God acting at creation, *And when they heard this, they lifted their voices to God with one accord and said, "O Lord, it is You who made the heaven and the earth and the sea, and all that is in them* (Acts 4:24). Through their prayer, they exalted the name of the God of creation.

Prayer brings you into conscious awareness of the contemporary present. Prayer brought the early believers into a conscious awareness of God acting at the crucifixion of Jesus, *For truly in this city there were gathered together against Your holy servant Jesus, whom You anointed, both Herod and Pontius Pilate, along with the Gentiles and the peoples of Israel* (Acts 4:27). Through their prayer, they exalted the name of God even at the crucifixion of Jesus.

Prayer brings you into a conscious awareness of the majestic future. Prayer brought the early believers into a conscious awareness of God acting within their predestinated future, *to do whatever Your hand and Your purpose predestined to occur. And now, Lord, take note of their threats, and grant that Your bond-servants may speak Your word with all confidence, while You extend Your hand to heal, and signs and wonders take place through the name of Your holy servant Jesus* (Acts 4:28-30). Through their prayer, they expected the nurture of God.

Knowledge of Scripture enhanced their prayer. Had they not known what God had done, how could they have prayed with such confidence? Had they not known Scripture, they would've had no idea what God would do. No doubt they would have feared the officials.

> **Prayer brings you into a consulting alliance with God.**

Prayer demands faith and requires an application of faith. Therein you consciously visualize so that you can consciously verbalize. A conscious awareness of God in the past, present and future propels you with courage and confidence through the issues of life.

Consulting Alliance

Prayer brings you into a consulting alliance with God. God rules the universe, but does so in consultation with those who pray. When you pray you work with God in ruling of the universe.

Prayer exercises great power within the universe. As a believer, God grants you this dynamic force. Jesus asked the blind beggar Bartimaeus, *What do you want Me to do for you?* (Mark 10:51). He gave Bartimaeus the privilege of ruling in the universe with Him.

The believers asked God to be aware of what the enemy was doing to them (Acts 4:29). Not to just notice, but to help them overcome their confrontation (Acts 4:30). God concerned Himself with the welfare the Israelites and the believers. Likewise, He concerns Himself with your circumstances as well.

Ask God about what is hassling you today. Tell Him what things need to improve quickly. Ask for the wisdom and courage to endure and make it happen, and to grant you the power to overcome your adversaries.

As you do this, you cooperate in a consulting alliance with the Heavenly Father. You're asking Him to take note of you and to give you the power to speak the word with boldness. Don't stop there. Tell God not only what to do towards those who are your enemy, but also what you want Him to do for you. This is consistent with what the believers did in Acts 4:30.

Focused Prayer

When you pray specifically focused prayers, you can easily see God's answers. Immediately, God did exactly what the believers asked in Acts 4:31. Their prayers brought them not only into a conscious awareness of God, but also into a consulting alliance with Him.

C.S. Lewis believed that through prayer God gives to man a part in Divine causality. Yet, prayer is not a matter of getting your will done in heaven but God's will done on earth.

Prayer is one of your most powerful spiritual services. God is waiting for you to ask Him to do some great things. Do your requests to the Lord challenge Him into His greatness?

Thought-provokng Questions

1. How is prayer a spiritual service?

2. How does prayer bring you into a conscious awareness of God?

3. How does prayer bring you into a consulting alliance with God?

Chapter Twelve

Intercessory Prayers

12

INTERCESSORY PRAYERS

Now I urge you, brethren, by our Lord Jesus Christ and by the love of the Spirit, to strive together with me in your prayers to God for me, that I may be rescued from those who are disobedient in Judea, and that my service for Jerusalem may prove acceptable to the saints; so that I may come to you in joy by the will of God and find refreshing rest in your company. Now the God of peace be with you all. Amen.

(Rom. 15:30-33)

The apostle Paul understood the value of intercessory prayer. Intercessory prayers are those prayed by an individual or a group, for another individual or group (Rom. 8:26, 27, 34; Num. 21:7). When you pray for someone else, you are interceding on his or her behalf. Likewise, when you ask someone else to pray for you, you are asking him or her to intercede on your behalf.

The apostle Paul asked the saints at Rome to pray, urging them to pray with him and for him: *Now I urge you, brethren, by our Lord Jesus Christ and by the love of the Spirit, to strive together with me in your prayers to God for me* (Rom. 15:30). Obviously, Paul prayed for himself before he invited others to join him.

Paul used an athletic term translated here as, *strive together with me*. It described the action of a team of athletes who join their forces together in a struggle against an opponent. The game tug-of-war illustrates this concept well.

Paul knew that opposing forces confronted him, and that alone he could do little. Through prayer united with other believers, he could accomplish much. Intercessory prayers create synergy.

Pray for Physical Safety

You may ask others to pray for your physical safety like Paul did: *that I may be rescued from those who are disobedient in Judea, and that my service for Jerusalem may prove acceptable to the saints* (Rom. 15:31). Paul expected to confront unbelievers in Judea that could and would hinder him and his mission. He wanted deliverance from them, so he asked the believers to pray for his safety from those in Judea.

To escape the hindering hands of the heathens in Judea only to die by the tearing tooth of a tiger while in route to Rome would be of little value to Paul and his mission. He needed not only deliverance *from* Judea but deliverance *to* Rome as well: *so that I may come to you in joy by the will of God and find refreshing rest in your company* (Rom. 15:32). Therefore, Paul asked the believers to pray for his safe arrival in Rome.

> **You may ask others to pray for your physical safety.**

Paul prayed for, and requested prayer for safety throughout the duration of his journey. You may ask for deliverance from and to as well.

Pray for Spiritual Service

Paul wanted physical safety so that he could render spiritual service acceptable to the saints in Rome (Rom. 15:31). Once again, here is a prayer for one thing so that something else may result. Prayers that result in spiritual service always find acceptance with God. When spiritual service is at stake, you may ask disciples to pray for your physical safety.

Paul urged the disciples to pray for acceptance of his service by the Jewish believers who lived in Jerusalem (Rom. 15:31). He asked the disciples to pray that God would restrict and remove the arrogant attitudes of the Jewish church, which might reject the service of Gentile disciples. This service consisted of a benevolent contribution offered to the saints in Jerusalem (Rom. 15:25-26; 2 Cor. 8:1-18).

It was likely that the Jews would feel superior to the Gentiles and reject their offering of help. However, we now know that the Jewish disciples did receive this offering (Acts 21:17-20; 24:17). Praise the Lord for the power of prayer.

Pray for Spiritual Servants

Paul urged believers to pray for acceptance of him as a servant (Rom. 15:32). He urged them to pray for acceptance of him for joy and refreshment in Rome. To escape the hindering hands of the heathens in Judea just to be rejected by the anguished attitudes of the saints in Jerusalem and Rome would be of little value. Therefore, he asked the disciples to ask God to restrict and remove the stingy attitudes that would cause believers to refuse to provide for his necessities (Rom. 15:24).

Your intercession is most powerful when you pray for others who are in covenant relationship with God. God called Moses to the mountain to speak with him (Exodus 31:18). While speaking with Moses, God informed him of His Sabbath as a sign of His covenant with the Israelites:

> *The Lord spoke to Moses, saying, But as for you, speak to the sons of Israel, saying, You shall surely observe My sabbaths; for this is a sign between Me and you throughout your generations, that you may know that I am the Lord who sanctifies you.*
>
> (Exodus 31:12-13)

Moses received the two tablets of stone upon which the finger of God had written the Ten Commandments. The finger of God is not physical entity of flesh and blood, but is equivalent to the spirit of God (Luke 11:20, Matt. 12:28).

Being fearful because Moses was away for a while, the Israelites made themselves an idol by fashioning the gold of their jewelry into a calf so they could worship it as their god (Exodus 32:1-6). Thus, they violated the covenant they had agreed to honor (Exodus 20 & 24).

This idolatrous violation angered God so He decided to

> **Your intercession is powerful when you pray for those in covenant with God.**

destroy them (Exodus 32:7-10). But, Moses interceded for them, and His intercessions persuaded God to change His mind (Exodus 32:11-14).

Intercession for Non-believers

Your intercession is powerful when you pray for those in covenant with God. However, it is also powerful when you stand in the gap for those who are *not* in covenant relationship with God.

To prevent strife, Abraham and his nephew, Lot, separated their herds. Lot chose the valley of the Jordan toward the wicked cities of Sodom and Gomorrah (Gen. 13:1-13). Some time later, the stench of wanton perversity and homosexuality called forth the wrath of God upon the cities.

God decided to inform Abraham of his intentions (Gen. 18:16-21), but Abraham interceded for the cities. Because of Abraham's intercession, God would have spared the wicked multitudes in the cities if only ten righteous ones had been found (Gen. 18:22-33).

The intercession of God's covenant people powerfully influences the mind of God. Surrender neither saints nor sinners to satanic devastations. Intercede for them.

Intercessory Prayer Can Restore Communities

Recently, a tornado tore through my hometown of Jackson, Tennessee, killing several people. The storm destroyed the worship facility of the East Jackson Church of Christ, where I formerly served as minister. It also demolished the house that we lived in while I served that church.

This tragedy caused suffering on two levels: individual and community. Individuals may focus on their immediate problems, but the communal suffering saturates a broader spectrum. However, because of the synergy created by numerous prayers, the community will heroically work to erase the face of this disaster.

Hurricane Hugo struck in 1989, and a church in Charleston, South Carolina had to reschedule one of my preaching appointments. The hurricane took the roof right off their building. Likewise, in 1991 a church in Selmer, Tennessee had to reschedule my preaching appointment when a tornado removed their roof. In both cases, the community synchronized its energies and recovered. From these disasters, we learn that through intercessory prayer communities can recover.

Thought-provoking Questions

1. What does intercessory prayer do for the one who prays?

2. What does intercessory prayer do for those who are interceded for?

3. How does intercessory prayer generate more spiritual momentum than isolated prayer?

CHAPTER THIRTEEN

Pray Before Deciding

13 PRAY BEFORE DECIDING

It was at this time that He went off to the mountain to pray, and He spent the whole night in prayer to God. And when day came, He called His disciples to Him and chose twelve of them, whom He also named as apostles: Simon, whom He also named Peter, and Andrew his brother; and James and John; and Philip and Bartholomew; and Matthew and Thomas; James the son of Alphaeus, and Simon who was called the Zealot; Judas the son of James, and Judas Iscariot, who became a traitor.

(Luke 6:12-16)

Though Jesus was knowledgeable and powerful, He depended on an extensive prayer life for energy, spending entire nights praying to His Father:

> *It was at this time that He went off to the mountain to pray, and He spent the whole night in prayer to God.*
>
> (Luke 6:12)

On this occasion, from among Jesus' disciples, He selected twelve men naming them as apostles.

The word *apostle* means *one who had been commissioned to represent another*. Jesus selected the twelve apostles to represent Him in ministry. However, intense prayer preceded His decision.

Pray First

Sufficient spiritual meditation should precede all of your major decisions. Supreme benefits rise from the bed of sufficient spiritual meditation. Spiritual meditation clears your vision of chronological issues.

Timing is often crucial for your success, like the timing of your heartbeat is crucial to good health. Some time ago, a friend discovered that he had an irregular heartbeat. The doctors decided to stop his heart and return it to a proper schedule. This is scary just talking about it.

Timing is not as crucial in all situations, but it is important. For example:

- Should we get married this year or wait till next year?

- Should we have a child now or wait till next year?

- Should I go to graduate school now, or go next year?

> **Sufficient spiritual meditation should precede all of your major decisions.**

- Should I get involved in evangelism now or get involved next year?

People spend much of their life agonizing over decisions. However, making decision without prayer is akin to traveling without a map.

Jesus had been training His disciples for a while and He needed to name some apostles, but at the right time. He knew through prayer that it was time to select the twelve and set them apart.

Sufficient spiritual meditation clarifies your vision of personnel issues. Jesus called many disciples, but needed to deputize only twelve as apostles.

- Who would He choose?

- What criteria would He use?

- How will those chosen feel?

- How will those not chosen feel?

- How will this affect the cohesion of the team and the future ministry?

These questions are very important, so Jesus dared not decide without prayer. Then, after He prayed, the decision was made. What a marvelous pattern for you.

Personnel issues are important. Have you ever hired the wrong person? Chosen the wrong confidant?

After Jesus spent the night in prayer, He no doubt looked at those around Him clearly knowing whom to select. The infinite wisdom of God empowered Jesus and gave Him clear perspective, thus enabling Him to select the right disciples. There was no doubt in His mind that He was deputizing the right men.

> **If the decision is worth making, it's worth praying about.**

Sufficient spiritual meditation clarifies your vision of numerical issues as well. Have you ever failed to hire enough people or have hired too many? Ask God, How many employees do I need?

Likewise, when you are planning your family. Ask God, How many children should we have?

Someone said that rich people are afraid that poor people are going to steal their resources and that poor people are afraid that rich folk are going to hoard all of the resources. There is always a resource issue. Do you have enough? Do you have enough set aside for retirement? Do you have enough life insurance or enough hospitalization insurance? Do you have enough money for your education?

How often we agonize over having enough. Sometimes we go through it every week.

If the decision is worth making, it's worth praying about. You shouldn't make major decisions without spending sufficient time in prayer. You may wonder how much time is necessary to pray, so pray until there's no doubt in your mind that you clearly see the course of action to take.

Wait till you have a clear perspective. Then you can move through life with zeal and zest. This is possible when sufficient spiritual meditation precedes your major decisions.

Thought-provoking Questions

1. How does prayer help clarify your vision of chronological issues?

2. How does prayer help clarify your vision of personnel issues?

3. How does prayer help clarify your vision of numerical issues?

CHAPTER FOURTEEN
PRAYING IN THE SPIRIT

14 Praying in the Spirit

With all prayer and petition pray at all times in the Spirit, and with this in view, be on the alert with all perseverance and petition for all the saints, and pray on my behalf, that utterance may be given to me in the opening of my mouth, to make known with boldness the mystery of the gospel, for which I am an ambassador in chains; that in proclaiming it I may speak boldly, as I ought to speak.

(Eph. 6:18-20)

The apostle Paul challenged the saints to pray in the spirit, *And take the helmet of salvation, and the sword of the Spirit, which is the word of God. With all prayer and petition pray at all times in the*

Spirit, and with this in view, be on the alert with all perseverance and petition for all the saints (Eph. 6:17-18). To pray in the spirit is to pray in obedience to the direction of the Holy Spirit.

Spirit and Sword

Paul draws a parallel using the Spirit and a sword, but also connects the Spirit with prayer. This literary connection signifies that the sword of the Spirit works in unison with prayer in the Spirit.

God expects the saints to pray when attacked by the devil. However, He never intended for you to substitute prayer for performance. Don't stop doing as you are praying. Pray for a job, but keep on searching. Pray for peace but keep on learning how to promote peace. God expects you to pray concurrently with your performance. When Satan attacks, pray while you resist (James 5:7).

> **To pray in the spirit is to pray in obedience to the direction of the Holy Spirit.**

Stephen preached a cutting sermon to some cruel people as recorded in Acts 6:8-7:54. Indeed, they were of Satan in their opposition. In the midst of the satanic opposition, Stephen visualized the glory of God and Jesus standing in the presence and power of God (Acts 7:55). Then he verbalized what he had visualized, *and he said, Behold, I see the heavens opened up and the Son of Man standing at the right had of God* (Acts 7:56). Stephen only spoke after seeing, and only told what he saw. *They went on stoning Stephen as he called on the Lord and said, "Lord Jesus, receive my spirit* (Acts 7:59). Stephen asked the Lord to receive his spirit only after he saw Jesus paying attention to what was going on.

See the Dynamics

If you haven't the faith to see the spiritual dynamics, there is little or nothing you can say. You cannot verbalize your faith until after you have visualized your faith.

Stephen asked God to forgive those who stoned him. He could pray for forgiveness because he saw a God that would forgive.

> *Then falling on his knees, he cried out with a loud voice, Lord, do not hold this sin against them! Having said this, he fell asleep.*
> (Acts 7:60)

Praying in the spirit energizes your spiritual muscles. When you pray you activate and energize the spiritual might and energy that God has placed at your disposal.

Pray at all times for all situations. You do this by verbalizing your faith at all times, in all situations. However, before you say, you must see. Praying at all times for all situations forces you to see things by faith, at all times in all situations.

Spiritual insight allows one person to see and say more than another. You can't simply speak what another says. You must say according to the sight of your faith.

You should only say about a situation what God has revealed about it. Therefore, before you pray ask God what He says. Ask Him what principles of Scripture address the situation.

When you pray for a sick person, you should say what God said: *Beloved, I pray that in all respects you may prosper and be in good health, just as your soul prospers* (3 John 1:2). God said that He wants believers to enjoy good health. Therefore, you should never pray for health and say If it be your will. Now you know it's God's will. You should only pray, If it be Thy will concerning matters about which God has not specifically spoken.

The Will of God

Good health conforms to the ideal will of God. However, God will permit your health to deteriorate. Entering the Promised Land conformed to the ideal will of God. However, did all who left

Egypt enter Canaan? No. God permitted some to die in the wilderness, because death in the wilderness conformed to the permissive will of God. The ideal will and the permissive will of God are sometimes different.

God's ideal will is for all to be saved, *This is good and acceptable in the sight of God our Savior, who desires all men to be saved and to come to the knowledge of truth* (1 Tim. 2:3-4). Yet, He permits some to be lost and ignorant of the truth.

> **Praying in the spirit energizes your spiritual muscles.**

Praying expresses your faith and convictions on the revealed will of God. Therefore, you shouldn't pray, If it be Thy will if God has said it's His will.

James addressed prayer by writing, *But if any of you lacks wisdom, let him ask of God, who gives to all generously and without reproach, and it will be given to him* (James 1:5). But isn't there a verse that says, If it be thy will? What about James 4:13-15?

> *Come now, you who say, Today or tomorrow we will go to such and such a city, and spend a year there and engage in business and make a profit. Yet you do not know what your life will be like tomorrow. You are just a vapor that appears*

for a little while and then vanishes away. Instead, you ought to say, If the Lord wills, we will live and also do this or that.

James was speaking of a situation about which God has not specifically spoken. God has not specifically given all the details of the future. He hasn't revealed to you what economic ventures you will engage in tomorrow. Therefore, in this instance, you should say, If it be your will.

Not only should you always pray for all situations, but you should always pray for all the saints. Notice again, *With all prayer and petition pray at all times in the Spirit, and with this in view, be on the alert with all perseverance and petition for all the saints* (Eph. 6:18). You should pray general prayers for all the saints for their basic necessities.

Pray Specific Prayers

Also pray for the specific needs of the saints. The word petition means praying a special kind of prayer. Move beyond general prayers and pray specific prayers for all the saints. However, before you can pray for their specific needs, you must know their specific needs.

For example, I received a call from a fellow believer who asked me to pray for his business. I asked him to give me some particulars. I wanted to know specifically what to pray for.

He told me that he was in business with several partners, and they wanted to dissolve the business. He said they need an equitable procedure for closing down.

Without being told these specifics, I could have only prayed a general prayer for him. I would never have imagined that he wanted me to pray for the dissolution of his business. Most likely I would have prayed for the prosperity of his business. But rather than needing prosperity, he needed a procedure.

To pray for specific needs, you must keep current with the status of the needs. Suppose you receive a prayer request to pray for the family of a terminally ill grandmother. Very likely you would pray for the comforting strength and cohesion of that family in addition to the health of the grandmother. You may also pray for compassion and medical wisdom to flourish in the hearts and minds of the medical attendants.

Two weeks later the grandmother dies. Shouldn't the specifics of your prayers change? The former prayer for medical wisdom is outdated. Some will say, God knows and understands. Exactly! God knows that you should think enough of prayer to remain current.

Prayer Energizes Your Spiritual Muscles

Prayer energizes your spiritual muscles. Before closing your eyes and opening your mouth to pray, recall what God has said about the situations for which you are going to pray. Then pray consistently with what God has revealed.

When you ask others to pray for you, give them your specific requests. The apostle Paul requested prayer for himself, look at what he asked for, *and pray on my behalf, that utterance may be given to me in the opening of my mouth, to make known with boldness the mystery of the gospel* (Eph. 6:19). Paul asked the believers to pray that God would tell him what to say and that he might say it courageously when the opportunity presented itself.

If you aren't a Christian and haven't committed yourself to God, why do you pray? You may say, God is good to me, He takes care of me, just like He takes care of you. Great! That's another good reason why you ought to become a Christian! The goodness of God attracts, *Or do you think lightly of the riches of His kindness and tolerance and patience, not knowing that the kindness of God leads you to repentance* (Rom. 2:4)?

Thought-provoking Questions

1. Why do you need to pray if you are looking for work?

2. Why does one person see things differently in the spirit than another?

3. How is it that good health conforms to the will of God, yet He allows people to become sick and die?

CHAPTER FIFTEEN

PRAYING THROUGH YOUR ADDICTIONS

15
PRAYING THROUGH YOUR ADDICTIONS

For this reason I bow my knees before the Father, from whom every family in heaven and on earth derives its name, that He would grant you, according to the riches of His glory, to be strengthened with power through His Spirit in the inner man, so that Christ may dwell in your hearts through faith; and that you, being rooted and grounded in love, may be able to comprehend with all the saints what is the breadth and length and height and depth, and to know the love of Christ which surpasses knowledge, that you may be filled up to all the fullness of God. Now to Him who is able to do far more abundantly beyond all that we ask or think, according to the power that works within us, to Him be the glory in the church and in Christ Jesus to all generations forever and ever. Amen.

(Eph. 3:14-21)

This chapter will help you digest and assimilate the Word of God through prayer, and obtain the stamina needed to successfully resist the demons of drug addiction or any other addiction. Implement these practical procedures, assimilate the food (Word) of God, and develop the stamina to permanently overthrow your devastating addictions.

Procedure

Before you start

1. Select three accountable and uncompromising disciples of Christ to whom you will give total authority to manage your recovery program. You must be totally accountable to these three (3) disciples for all your thoughts and actions twenty-four (24) hours per day, seven (7) days per week, for the next fifty (50) days. They will have the right to encourage and/or rebuke you for any and all behavior.

2. Write the names of fifty (50) positive people who support you in overcoming your addiction and who will serve as a daily prayer partner for you.

3. Write the names of fifty (50) negative people who benefit from your addiction and/or dont want you to overcome your addiction.

4. Plan your victory celebration for the fiftieth (50th) day after beginning your program.

After you start
1. Each day, write a victory letter to a different one of the positive people on your list. Ask them to respond to your letter if they chose to do so. Keep each letter in a blue three-ring pocket folder. You may add to each letter and resend it any time after it has been written.

2. Ask each one of your positive people to pray daily for your recovery.

3. Invite each of the fifty (50) positive people to celebrate with you at your victory party. At the celebration party give and/or read the letters to each positive person. Mail letters to those who are unavailable to attend.

4. Each day, write a victory letter to a different one of the negative people on your list. Tell them that you are overcoming your addiction and will never again allow them to influence you negatively. Inform them that you will be limiting your fellowship

with them unless they want to become a positive person and participate in your recovery. Mail each of these letters the day that you write them.

5. Have no fellowship with any of the negative people on your list for the next fifty (50) days.

Power

God has an incredible investment of Himself in you. Therefore, as a disciple of Christ, you are a powerful person. Through appropriate prayer and power exercises, you can break Satans stronghold and recover from the addictive rut of ruin.

Earnest prayer will help enable you to capture your victory, *The effective prayer of a righteous man can accomplish much* (James 5:16b). A focused prayer life will activate the elements necessary to produce strength for overcoming any and every addiction.

However, prayer by itself never produces stamina. Just as eating by itself never produces strength. Only after food has been digested and assimilated in the body does it produce strength. Only after the food (Word) of God has been digested and assimilated in the individual does it build stamina, *Therefore, putting aside all malice and all deceit and hypocrisy and envy and all slander, like newborn babies, long for the pure milk of the word, so that by it you may grow in respect to salvation* (1 Peter 2:1-2).

Only to the extent that prayer causes digestion and assimilation of the Word of God can it build stamina. Therefore, pray for a thorough digestion and assimilation of Gods Word.

PRAYER: What?
Follow the prayer model of chapter seven (7).

PRAYER: What happens?
Make a vow with God to participate in the application of your prayer (Numbers 21:1-3; 30; 1-2). He who prays, but doesn't act on what he knows, is like the man who plans, but never sows!

PRAYER: Where?
Choose a certain place to pray like Jesus did:

> *But Jesus Himself would often slip away to the wilderness and pray.*
>
> (Luke 5:16)

> *And it happened that while He was praying alone, the disciples were with Him, and He questioned them, saying, Who do the people say that I am?*
>
> (Luke 9:18)

> *Some eight days after these sayings, He took along Peter and John and James, and went up on the mountain to pray.*
>
> (Luke 9:28)

> *It happened that while Jesus was praying in a certain place, after He had finished, one of His disciples said to Him, "Lord, teach us to pray just as John also taught his disciples.*
>
> (Luke 11:1)

Decide where you will pray each day—you may utilize several places. You can take a positive person with you from time to time. However, it is better to go alone.

PRAY: When?

Designate a certain period of time for prayer. Immediately after arising from sleep each day, before going to work or school, or prior to participating in any other mind consuming distraction are preferable.

Before proceeding to pray, decide how long you will pray. Jesus spent all night in prayer, *It was at this time that He went off to the mountain to pray, and He spent the whole night in prayer to God* (Luke 6:12). Jesus chided the disciples for being unable to spend even one hour in prayer, *And He came to the disciples and found them sleeping, and said to Peter, So, you men could not keep watch with Me for one hour?* (Matt. 26:40). One hour may be the bare minimum needed to develop strength to overcome your disastrous struggle with addiction.

Fasting

Prayer coupled with fasting energizes your strength and can be a source of awesome power to break addictions. Jesus made a promise to reward those who fast, though many seem to not care: *...your father who sees what is done in secret will reward you* (Matt. 6:16-18).

Jesus speaks of this spiritual discipline twice in His recorded ministry. The first time He says not if but when you fast (Matt. 6:16-18), assuming that His people will practice fasting. His concern is how it will be done. The second time He says, when they will fast (Matt. 9:15), seeming to know that His disciples would fast.

Fasting can be an empty ritual, but when done properly is a channel of divine power that takes your prayers to another level. Fasting intensifies the cry of your heart toward God.

Jehoshaphat called on Judah to fast and pray for deliverance (2 Chron. 20:1-17). The king of Ninevah called for a citywide fast to avert the judgment of God (Jonah 3:6-9). Esther summoned the Jews to fast before she approached the king (Esther 4:15-17). Ezra called on Gods people to fast and pray for protection (Ezra 8:21). Nehemiah called on Jerusalem to fast and pray (Neh. 1:4). Church leaders fasted and sought Gods direction for their ministry (Acts 13:1-3). Paul and Barnabas prayed as they appointed elders (Acts 14:23). God even authorized a husband and wife to abstain from sexual intimacy in order to fast and pray (1 Cor. 7:1-5). It's an awesome privilege to fast and pray!

Thought-provoking Truths

1. Addictions can be broken.

2. Prayer enables the person to break the cycle of addiction.

3. Addictions must be broken to fulfill God's plan for your life.

Epilogue

Things You Should Know

Faith is what you do about what you believe that God indeed does sanction (2 Cor. 4:13).

Faithful is the fulfillment of your assigned responsibilities (Col. 4:7-9).

Fellowship is compatible participation in a compatible activity because of compatible interest (1 John 1:1-10).

Love an attitude and an action caused by a need but regulated by relationship and resources (1 John 3:16-17).

Prayer is verbalization of the visualization of your faith (Acts 4:23-31).

Sin is your heart when opposed to the will of God (Acts 5:3-4, 8:20-22; Matt. 15:1-20).

Worship is the expression of your pledge of allegiance to God.

Things You Should Do

Because of, and by the blood of Jesus, you can be forgiven of sin. The blood of Christ cleanses you from the guilt of sin as you are born into the family of God. Only through Jesus Christ can you enjoy a saved relationship with God. Jesus declared that He is the only way to the Father (John 14:6).

Hear

Through Jesus Christ, salvation, the deliverance from the penalty of sin, is available for you (John 6:44-45). You must hear the gospel, which is the good news that Jesus Christ became the sacrifice for your sin (1 Cor. 15:1-4).

The book of Acts contains many conversion stories. Preceding each conversion, the disciples preached Jesus Christ and Him crucified to the lost audience (Acts 2:36, 8:5, 35).

Believe

For the gospel to be of benefit, you must believe the message (Acts 15:7). Unless you believe, you will never become converted (Heb. 4:1-2).

Repent

Repent. Change your mind, purpose, opinion, moral thought, reflection, behavior and attitude (Acts 17:30; Luke 13:3-5).

Confess

The word, *confess*, means to acknowledge, to admit, or to agree with. You must agree with God that indeed Jesus Christ is His Son (Acts 8:37).

Be Baptized

Baptism is your burial in water and resurrection in Christ, and is done in response to your faith in Jesus Christ as the Son of God (Acts 8:12, 37-39; 1 Peter 3:21).

ABOUT THE AUTHOR

John Marshall has given more than 2,000 presentations throughout the United States, helping thousands of people with his practical and penetrating teaching style. He is an author, editor, media producer, facilitator for conflict resolution, motivational speaker, preacher, public relations director, teacher, trainer, and relationship consultant. He received his bachelor's degree from Freed-Hardeman University, master's degree in counseling from Theological University of America, and has done additional graduate work at University of Memphis and Southern Christian University. He is a staff writer for The Christian Echo and The Revivalist magazine, a member of the Alumni Advisory Board of Freed-Hardeman University, and preaches for Graceview Church of Christ in Stone Mountain, Georgia, where he and his family live.

OTHER BOOKS BY JOHN MARSHALL

Final Answer:
You Asked, God Answered

God Knows!
There Is No Need to Worry

Good and Angry
A Personal Guide to Anger Management

My God !
Who He Is Will Change Your Life

The Power of the Tongue
What You Say Is What You Get

Success Is a God Idea

Show Me the Money
7 Exercises That Build Economic Strength

Contact Information

For further information about John Marshall, his ministry, and other ministry resources, please contact him at

Mail:
John Marshall
P. O. Box 878
Pine Lake Georgia 30072

Web:
www.graceview.us

Email:
jdm@graceview.us

Phone:
(404) 297-9050
(404) 316-5525